Noah's Ark

Written by Laurie Lazzaro Knowlton

Illustrated by Roberta Collier-Morales

Noah listened to God.

Noah built the ark.

Noah called the animals.

Noah gathered the food.

8 Noah watched and waited.

Noah sent a raven.

Noah sent a dove.

Noah waited for sun.

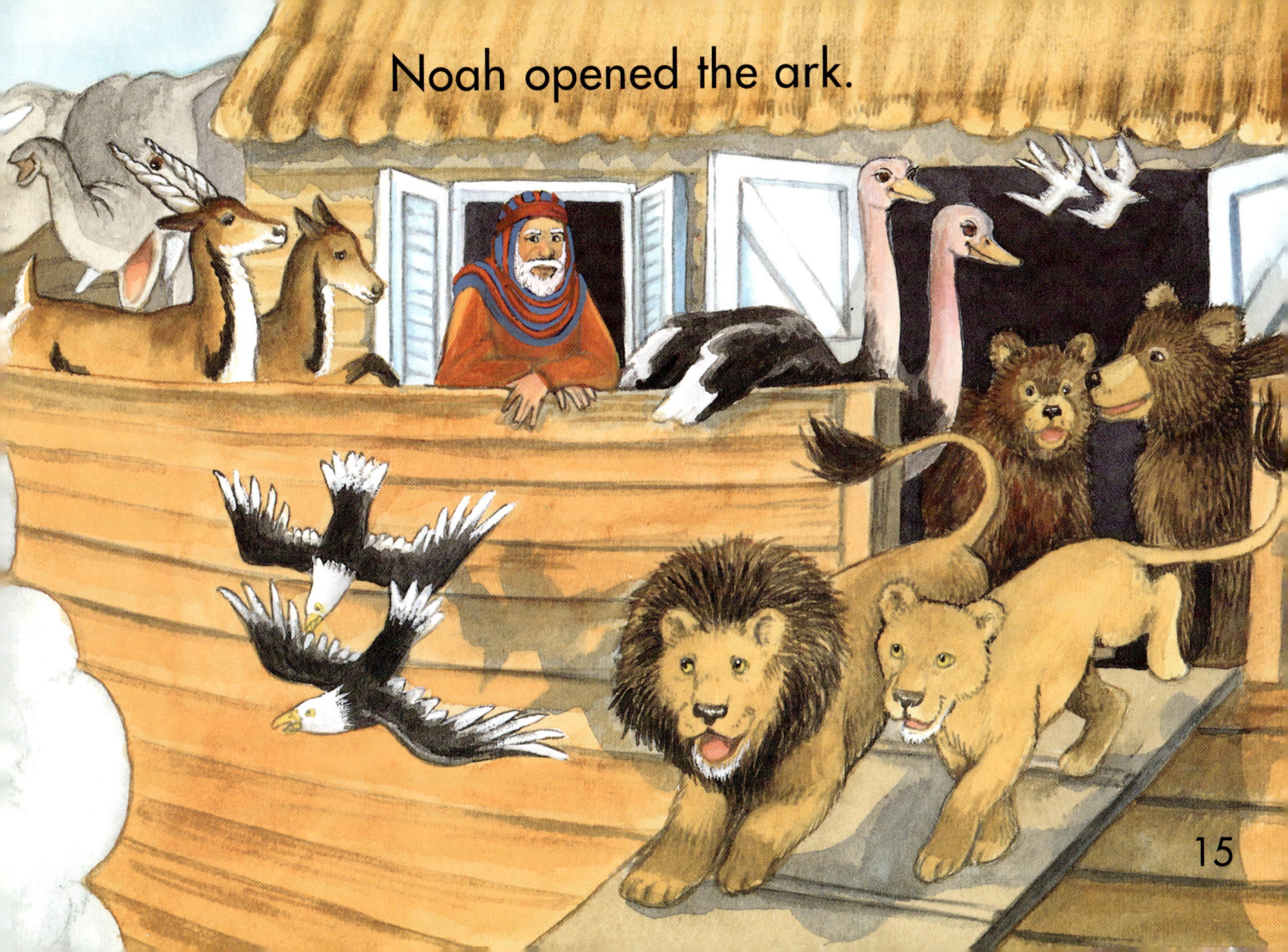

Noah knelt and rejoiced.

Emergent Readers for Little Believers

Two by Two

Written by Susan and Steven Traugh
Illustrated by Andra Chase

The ducks came

two by two.

The pigs came

two by two.

The sheep came

two by two.

The alligators came

two by two.

The giraffes came

two by two.

The lions came

two by two.

The elephants came . . . oh no!

Whew!

The elephants came . . . one, THEN two!